Pandemic Dreams

Also by Deirdre Barrett:

The Pregnant Man: Tales from a Hypnotherapist's Couch

The Committee of Sleep: How Artists, Scientists, and Athletes Use their Dreams for Creative Problem Solving—and How You Can Too

Supernormal Stimuli: How Primal Urges Overran Their Evolutionary Purpose

Trauma and Dreams (Editor)

Pandemic Dreams

by Deirdre Barrett

Cover image: *Help, I can't wake up!* by Deirdre Barrett

Published by Oneiroi Press

IBSN 978-0-9828695-3-6

Table of Contents

Introduction

I looked down at my stomach and saw dark blue stripes. I "remembered" these were the first sign of being infected with COVID-19.

My spaceship was supposed to be heading back to earth but it got diverted to Saturn, and I ended up just living there alone.

My home was a Covid-19 test center. People weren't wearing masks. I'm taken aback because I wasn't asked to be a test site. I'm worried that my husband and son (who actually lives out of state) will catch it because of my job as a healthcare worker.

I was a giant antibody. I was so angry about covid-19 that it gave me superpowers, and I rampaged around attacking all the virus I could find. I woke so energized!

Since the covid-19 pandemic swept around the world, and we began to shelter-in-place, people have reported unusually active dream lives. We're remembering more dreams than usual, and those dreams are especially vivid and bizarre. The virus itself is the star of many--literally or in one of its metaphoric guises.

As a dream researcher at Harvard Medical School, I was immediately curious to see what our dream lives would tell us about our deepest reactions to this new disaster. I had studied the dreams of 9/11 survivors, of Kuwaitis during the first Gulf War, and dreams from POWs in WWII concentration camps. What patterns from these past crises would we see again? What dream metaphors would be unique to the current pandemic? And most important, how might a better understanding of our collective dream lives help us as we move through this crisis, and beyond?

In late March, I began to collect dream reports via an online survey. The response to this has been overwhelming. In less than three months, I have already collected more than 9,000 dreams from over 3,700 dreamers, all around the world.

Pandemic Dreams discusses why our dreams have been so vivid since this began, and explores different forms the crisis is taking in our dreamlife—characterizing major themes in these dreams and what they symbolize. It offers guidance on how we can best utilize our newly supercharged dream lives to aid us through the crisis and beyond. It explains practical exercises for dream interpretation, reduction of nightmares, and incubation of helpful, problem-solving dreams. It also examines the larger arena of what these collective dreams tell us about our instinctive, unconscious responses to the threat and how we might integrate them for more livable policies through these times.

Many of the book's generalizations and examples rely on my survey, but it also includes the longer conversations I've had with people about their dreams during the pandemic and draws on my past crisis dream collections for comparison. The book is divided into five chapters addressing different aspects of pandemic dreams; each ends with a practical exercise you can use with that category of dream.

Chapter I) The Year of Dreaming Vividly

Why Now?

> Is anybody else having really weird/vivid dreams during this whole lockdown or is it just me? @juustmolls

> I thought I had vivid dreams before but since quarantine they've been over the top realistic! @litesue

> This unique time is leaving me with really messed up dreams. Anyone else? @LizHump77

People are remembering more dreams than usual. Longer dreams. More vivid dreams. More bizarre dreams. A study by The Lyon Neuroscience Research Center found a 35% increase in dream recall between the third week of March and the third week of April. Twitter and Instagram posts with hashtags like #coronadreams #covid19dreams #quarantinedreaming and #pandemicnightmares have gone viral.

Any major event stirs up our dreams—and if it's a crisis, it stirs more anxiety into the mix. We're thinking more intensely and emotionally by day, and I believe *dreams are just thinking in a different biochemical state,* so of course our dreams are also more intense and emotional. I saw a surge in vivid dreams after 9/11 and in the other crisis samples I've examined.

However, the period we are living through is unique in the shared dreamlife of humanity.

Most crises are accompanied by less sleep: people have trouble dozing off because of worry or having to do extra tasks to protect themselves.

People in the modern world are typically a bit sleep deprived. We don't sleep until our bodies would naturally awaken. Instead, we set an alarm, pour caffeine into ourselves, and rush off to work or school. Evenings have wide array of social possibilities and family responsibilities, Normally, if one has trouble falling asleep or awakens in the middle of the night, you get less sleep. This one is different. Now, one can sleep in later or take afternoon naps. One Facebook meme characterizes the difference:

> Past generations have been asked to march off to war and die. In this war, we're being asked to lay on our couch in pajamas and watch Netflix. We can handle this.

The vast majority of dreams happen during rapid eye movement (REM) sleep, and we go into REM sleep every 90 minutes. If someone sleeps in a sleep lab for eight hours and is awakened a few minutes into each REM period, they will generally recall five dreams that night. Our long-term memory is not turned on during REM sleep, so most dreams are forgotten because we don't wake up and activate the transfer into our long-term storage. Each REM period is longer than the last: just a few minutes at first and up to 30 minutes by the last one. Each gains more "REM density" which just means literally that the eyes move more intensely but it correlates with the vividness and bizarreness of the dreams. When you sleep six instead of eight hours, you don't lose one-fourth of your dream life—you lose almost half--and exactly the dreams that will be the most vivid, bizarre, and memorable. On the other hand, when we're catching up on sleep, we often have epic, wild dreams.

Finally, fewer people are setting alarms, so we wake up naturally which is usually out of REM sleep, whereas an alarm has an 80% chance of catching some other stage of sleep. Alarm clocks are the enemy of dream recall.

This combination of a global crisis and more time to sleep makes this an extraordinary time in the history of dreaming. Everything is converging to cause us to have more compelling dreams and to remember them more clearly.

One becomes interested in dreams when dreams are intense experiences. Some people are keeping a dream journal for the first time. It has never been so easy. We have more time to write them in handsome notebooks if we choose—perhaps illustrating them as well, but there are also now numerous apps that enable quickly dictating and storing them in neatly indexed texts.

Others are sharing their dreams with family and friends. When CNN's Sanjay Gupta interviewed me for his Coronavirus podcast, he said one reason he is interested in dreams during this time is that he'd overheard his two daughters sharing dreams in the morning. The older had dreamed of a line to get jobs on a beach; when she got to the front of the line, she was assigned the tasks of keeping secrets and of knitting bright yellow scarves. His younger daughter dreamed of an ominous lump under the covers of her bed; she jumped on it to attack and woke herself up screaming. They discussed these with each other and then with their father--nothing they'd had time for when rushing off to school in different grades. All around the world, people are sharing these newly vivid dreams to the families and friends they're sequestered with or in Zoom conversations. Facebook and Google Hangout are full of new online dream-sharing groups.

Action: Dream Sharing and Interpretation

Sharing our waking reactions to the pandemic is making people around the world feel closer, and sharing our dreamlife adds a deeper unconscious dimension to that. Recount your dreams to family or roommates—or remote Zoom buddies. Ask them about their recent dreams. You can simply share them as an important experience you've had or you can invite listeners to help you think about what they mean. Research finds that when a person shares dreams with listeners who pay deep attention, the listeners feel an enhanced sense of empathy.

Discussion of the meaning of the dream further leads to the dreamer experiencing gains in self-insight. Modern dream interpretation is not an "expert" telling someone what their dreams symbolize nor looking up content in an alleged "dream dictionary." Dream psychologists basically agree that the dreamer is the authority on their own metaphors and others can simply help them get to their own interpretation of their dream. Two of the most common techniques are Montague Ullman's Group Dreamwork Method and The Dream Interview developed by Gayle Delaney and Loma Flowers.

The Ullman Method works best with at least five or six people—enough to generate different perspectives on the dream. It approaches the dilemma of no one knowing definitively what another's dream may mean by having group members offer suggestions phrased, "If it were my dream . . ." and associating to dream elements from their own storehouse of experience. One interpretation may click for the dreamer with an "aha." Other times, a not-even-slightly-correct-for-this-dreamer suggestion may serve as a springboard for them to think, "No—it's more the opposite—it's that . . . ." Another step in the process involves asking clarifying questions such as "Is the coworker in the dream a real waking-life person?" or "Were you (dreamer) your current age in the dream?" Other queries are about context, "Had anything unusual happened during a real grocery trip?" or "Have you seen any waking life image like the purple aura surrounding the infected person?" The dreamer controls the process and says as much or as little as they want about what they're learning about the dream from trying on these associations.

In a recent Zoom session, UK psychologist Mark Blagrove led Ullman-style work with a dream of Mia Muliau, a health care worker originally from New

Zealand who is currently working in Australia. Mia dreamed of being inside a dark abalone shell as an ominous buzzing sound surrounded her. The sound abated, however, and she looked out and saw a bright ocean scene and darling seal pup. Mia identified with some interpretations of the imagery as addressing the pandemic: that AU and NZ had been every bit as frightened as anywhere when the pandemic appeared, that she'd originally needed protection which a shell is, but that things were "looking brighter" now that AU and NZ had escaped relatively unscathed and that the pup might represent health care workers getting a lot of love currently. She also identified with more personal suggestions that the seal pup was inviting her to "come out of her shell" and to be more playful—the dreamer characterized herself as generally very cautious and serious. [See Figure 1 for a painting artist Julia Lockheart made of Mia's dream on a page of *Freud's Interpretation of Dreams* during the session]

An almost opposite approach is taken with the Dream Interview. It works best in a dyad but the dreamer can also serve as their own interviewer. In this approach, the interviewer refrains from sharing any interpretations of their own. They ask non-leading questions about key elements of the dream—characters, objects, actions, and settings—and inquire about each in turn: "Pretend I'm from another planet—tell me what is a . . . ?" The mock-alien role doesn't need to be repeated with every question, but one continues to ask simply for basic descriptions. Interesting metaphors will pop out less self-consciously than if one were asking, "and what does this symbolize for you?" The interviewer inquires about any feelings

Figure 1: Julia Lockheart's painting of Mia Muliau's dream during Mark Blagrove's Ullman-style dreamwork on DreamsID.

about various elements if the dreamer didn't originally include any mention of emotions. Finally, they ask, "Is there anything in your waking life that is like . . . ?"

plugging in the most metaphoric elements of the descriptions to prompt connections and insights.

I did a dream interview with Andy Sarjahani about a dream of his for a short animated film produced by Time.com. Andy dreamed he was in Austin, Texas, where he'd spent his college years. He walked through his old neighborhood and found that a tourist bar was the only place open; but it was hopping, so he decided to go in. While waiting for his drink he was shocked to see a man standing next to him blow away. Looking to other people for their response, he realized they were all cardboard cut-outs who proceeded to flutter away in the wind.

Upon questioning, Andy said the only cardboard cutouts he could think of were in the film *Home Alone 2*. The child protagonist is isolated in his uncle's townhouse surrounded by a gang of criminals plotting to kidnap or kill him, and he orchestrates a fake party with cardboard cutout people passing by windows on pull strings.

In this case, it seemed almost redundant to perform the final step of inquiring, "Is there anything in your waking life that is like being a kid 'Home Alone' with only cardboard cutout people for company and safety?" However, with less blatant metaphors, this is often the stage where a dreamer gets a big "aha" upon hearing their associations repeated back within the framework of the dream. It's not uncommon for metaphors to contain pun-like imagery such as Andy's. [See Figure 2]

11

Figure 2: Still of Andy Sarjahani's dream from the upcoming short film produced by Kathleen Flynn and Margaret Cheatham Williams and animated by Maya Edelman; used with permission from Time.com.

Chapter 2) Fear of the Virus

I'm catching the virus!

> I have a reoccurring dream that we get a
> knock on our door and outside are people in
> hazmat suits. The door no longer opens
> because we haven't used it in so long. The
> hazmats tell us someone in our home has
> COVID-19 as confirmed by Parliament.
> Since were unable to get out, we are going
> to die of it.

A common category of dreams in my survey is simply
of catching the virus. Dreamers have trouble breathing
or spike a fever. Other symptoms are more dreamlike:
one woman sees a dark aura from a person she passes
on the street touch her body and knows that it has
infected her. Another looks down and notices bright
blue stripes on her stomach and remembers that's the
first sign of infection. Variations include one's children
or elderly parents coming down with the virus.

Dreamers may be tested for the disease. Many tests are
swabs much like the waking procedure. Others deviate
from real life:

> My husband and I are taking a test to see if
> we have the virus. They look just like those
> white plastic home-pregnancy tests. Both of
> us have a pink line—positive.

> I'm taking a COVID-19 test. But it's a sit-
> down multiple choice exam and I can't

figure out any of the answers. They tell me I failed and I have the disease.

Realizing one has the virus is often the end of the dream. Other times, it initiates a search for help. An array of attitudes toward the medical system play out on the dream stage. Some dreamers struggle endlessly to get to a hospital ("The streets in my town have changed; I don't recognize anything and people won't direct me—they just cough.") or try to get attention once there ("the medical staff was marching and staring straight ahead; I wondered if they had been replaced by androids"). Others locate a doctor or nurse who gives them an injection or pills to cure them. Many times it is more ambiguous: "I get a shot of something to relieve symptoms and potentially cure the disease but it's unclear if it will work."

Unconscious fears of doctors and of government show up in dreams of menace in the guise of aid:

> I'm about to be given a shot that will treat it, but I saw "cyanide" on the syringe and realized they were euthanizing everyone that had the virus.

> At the top of the escalator, they were giving a vaccine. But everyone who got vaccinated staggered away and died.

It's interesting to note what the particular dream scenario depicts about the dreamer's sense of vulnerability, their own efficacy, and the ability or willingness of healthcare professionals to help.

Mortuaries are another source of death-anxiety and a staple of horror film settings. One woman dreamed of evil morticians similar to other's depictions of doctors-as-villain:

> I am walking past a building and come to a white door with a sign which reads: "Only Self Embalming in Florida" (BTW....I live in New York).
> So, I walk in.
> I see a white bathtub with a gray liquid on the bottom and the man in the white lab coat says, "We dispose of the elders."
> I go through a door into the adjacent room and whatever was going on in there, I realized the Elders they were embalming and cremating were not dead yet.
> I ran out of there......and woke up!

A few dreamers are unafraid when they get the disease. They're using the possibility to play out practical plans. One mother dreams that she and her children all have the virus, denoted by white patches at the back of their throat. She calls her supervisor at work to say she will not be coming into the office for the next two weeks while they quarantine. She'd been wanting to work from home at the time of the dream. Another dream found an ingenious way to distance the dreamer from her fears:

> I was playing a Sims-like game, only it was more immersive, and in VR. There was a Sim who was me--she looked like me, had

my name. She was also in quarantine. She wandered around her house, being generally bored and looking for things to do. There was a sidebar of active effects and inventory. Suddenly, in that sidebar, there popped up a new effect: "COVID-19." My Sim was flushed. She started having trouble breathing. She fell to the floor, writhing, holding her throat, her chest. I watched as the little digital figure fought against the tightness in her chest, and she started sweating profusely. Then I woke up. Weirdly, it wasn't an anxiety dream. I'm sure the dream itself stemmed from my worries about the pandemic, but I had no emotional reaction to the dream itself.

Some dreams that seem to be about the pandemic, draw their imagery from science fiction:

After watching *Contagion*, I dream that I get COVID-19 and can physically feel myself suffocating, vision blacking out, physical pain. I know I'm dying.

. . . My friends were there in their *Outbreak* type PPE and I got upset that they had PPE and I didn't.

. . . and it's like that scene in *Pandemic* where trash has piled up . . .

We'll get to suggestions about managing anxiety dreams soon, but a heads-up now: bedtime streaming of disaster flicks about viruses devastating the planet won't make that list.

A final category of literal dreams about the virus dramatizes the necessary precautions for the dreamer. Any time we are learning new material, it is likely to show up in our dreams. This has been documented for everything from foreign languages to video games. Memory consolidation seems to be one of the tasks in which dreams play a role. In late March and April, people were learning to distance six feet apart, wear masks, and wash their hands and surfaces more than they ever had. Their dreams practiced these precautions. Dreamers might realize they aren't wearing masks and have come too close to someone. In other cases, the dreamers do everything perfectly but another character coughs on them or stands too close. The dream often starts in a blissfully pandemic-unaware world and remembering our current situation provides a motivating jolt:

> Recurring dream: I am in the process of trying to do something that is otherwise Important or responsible, like waiting in line to vote or holding my best friend 's brand new baby, and suddenly realize I'm not wearing a mask. I feel ashamed and dirty, and like I need to leave immediately, but I haven't yet done the thing I came there to do, and I leave feeling guilty about both.

> I take my elderly mother, aunt, and friend into a crowded mall. Suddenly I realize that

I forgot about the virus and nobody, including us, has masks on.

Early on in the pandemic, I dreamed that I ran into a European friend who gave me a double-cheek kiss greeting and then we both recoiled in horror and tried to figure out how to undo it.

I am in a packed restaurant, eating, laughing; I feel ebullient. I'm having drinks with my friends. We all reconvene in the restroom when I suddenly realize how dangerous the situation is. No masks! No social distancing! Too many people laughing and talking loudly right next to one another! I panic and try to explain but no one will listen to me. I'm frantic to get my friends to understand the danger repeatedly but they blow me off.

Some safety-practicing dreams are more surreal:

I'm at my chorus rehearsal. Several people are coughing. I feel it would be gauche to tell them they have the virus, so I just try to hold my breath as I sing.

When I woke up, all I could remember was that I'd done something wrong or violated a rule, and my punishment was having to shake an infinite line of hands.

I am at the sunny, yellow ballroom dance studio. No one else is around. I am stretching. Another me is tucked up in the corner, holding her (my) knees up to her chest. I and me have to maintain our distance from each other.

One young Australian woman who had completely ignored the early announcements of safety measures which she regarded as absurd had a dream that pointed out the necessity dramatically to her waking self:

> I had a dream that I threw a party after new restrictions were put in place, and a comically large amount of people attended. It felt very crowded, and I didn't realize how risky throwing a party is in these times was until later on in the dream, when Scott Morrison (Australian Prime Minister) sent out secret agents to bust people breaking the new isolation rules.

The dreamer said she awakened from the dream with a new appreciation that she had better attend to the health guidelines she'd been ignoring for the past week.

Bugs, Bugs, Bugs

> There was a tarantula that was somehow also COVID-19 coming thru the mail slot. (I have no mail slot)

I dreamt I had a roach infestation and that two of my friends had got it and one had died.

In one I remember very clearly, strange bugs (like a centipede or millipede) were released into a room where I was sleeping. We could only find one bug of many, so I was terrified to sleep until the other bugs were located.

Not all dreams about the virus are literal. After 9/11, I saw some metaphoric dreams. However, due to the dramatic images associated with that event, a majority dreamed of buildings falling, planes smashing into things and/or hijackers with knives. Our dreaming mind is intensely visual, so when it feels fear, it searches for an image to match that feeling. Bugs express what many are feeling about COVID-19. Swarms of flying insects--bees, hornets, wasps, gnats, horseflies—attack. Masses of toxic worms writhe in front of dreamers. Armies of cockroaches race toward them. Bedbugs, stink bugs. One woman dreamed of giant grasshoppers with vampire fangs.

They are the definitive metaphor now partly because of our slang use of the word "bug" to mean a virus or other illness, as in "I've got a bug." As I mentioned in the *Home Alone 2* cardboard cutouts example, dreams often represent words with visual images in pun-like fashion. At a deeper level, however, lots of tiny entities that cumulatively could harm or kill you makes a perfect metaphor for COVID-19.

Invisible Monsters

I dreamed they had started evacuating London but I was stuck there. I could see a "ghost" or "force" moving from one apartment to the other. It was possessing people and moving through them. Then it jumped from the building across onto my balcony and into me—that's when I woke up terrified.

. . . It was right behind me, breathing in low heaves and grabbing with invisible long fingers and hands. It was a dark, violent and hungry entity.

I'm with my family and lover and we're being chased by silent, almost invisible rats. I only see their tiny eyes and flashes of teeth behind us as we run.

Another metaphoric creature unique to this epidemic is the invisible monster. Some dreamers must cross exposed outdoor areas and know there are monsters that could kill them but which they can't spot. Others wander through building complexes and hear steps behind them or spot subtle shadows moving when they can't directly see the monsters. One woman dreamed that she was watching others being knocked down one by one. Terrible wounds appeared on their bodies until they died but she couldn't see the attacking creature. She remembered that it could jump to anyone within six feet after their former victim's death and realized *she was standing too close*. As with bugs, the invisible monsters haven't appeared after other crises but are unique to the elusive imagery of the coronavirus.

Invitations from the dead

> My mother and grandmother are deceased. At the beginning of the outbreak, they both came to me in my dream. I was totally surprised and happy to see them again. I asked why they were there and they said in unison, "We are here to get you." I knew what that meant and asked, "Now?" To which they both nodded yes. I said let me pack first, they smiled at each other, laughed and said, "you won't need anything". But they let me pack anyway. Instead of clothes, I picked up a photo frame that was showing movies of my life and memories with them. I laughed and cried and realized, it's been a good life but I was still hesitant to leave. They slowly walked out of the room and faded away. I knew I was supposed to follow them and headed for the door. I haven't dreamt about them or the virus since. I hope it was my fears manifesting themselves and not a sign of what is coming.

In *Death Shall Have No Dominion*, Charles Jackson observes, "The dead have largely lost their social importance, visibility, and impact in American society. Connection between the world of the dead and that of the living has been largely severed and the dead world is disappearing. It is a radical departure because for three centuries prior, life and death were not held apart." The dominion of the dead in dreams, however, has not diminished. The most distinctive characteristics of dreams include the breaching of waking logic, social taboos, and denial. Although modern trends may have decreased belief in the veracity of the dead returning in dreams, they have done nothing to stem their occurrence.

Dreams from the pandemic survey feature summons from the dead worthy of folktales. One woman is invited to break lockdown for a family picnic, but, upon arrival, discovers that the other attendees are the deceased branch of her family, rather than the living. Another dreamer arrives at a fancy party, and is offered a seat next to a corpse. A woman orders an Uber and a hearse arrives for her instead.

The loss of loved ones and desire to be with them again has people dreaming about the deceased in normal times. But currently news stories of ambulances carrying off people who are not seen by their families again or of bodies in refrigerated trucks parked outside hospitals and nursing homes stir up a new horror about mortality—and pandemic dreams are often about the immediate awareness that we could die of this.

One woman sees her deceased loved ones in a classic tunnel of light, but then she sees something else behind that vision:

> I dreamt I was having a near death experience. I was in a dark tunnel with a

light at one end. My dead relatives were there beckoning me towards the light. My mom said, "Come dear." I realized it wasn't really her, and I shouted, "That is not an expression my real mother would use--show your true selves!" The people turned into demonic vampire bats. They were biting a man who had died, and sucking out his memories. I could see hollow outlines of those already emptied floating at the end of the tunnel of light. I fled--presumably to the living.

Other metaphors for the virus

Any horrible event can be cast as the source of fear the dreamer feels about the invisible coronavirus:

This recurring dream started when COVID was becoming recognized as a pandemic. In the dream, I was with my family at the beach. I knew there was a tsunami coming because I could see the signs--the tide going out. I was trying to tell my family and they thought I was over-reacting. My son was particularly annoyed with me for ruining the vacation. I started telling strangers there was a tsunami coming and they ignored me, too. Finally a huge wave came in and battered the houses. I knew this was just the start so I was trying to round up my family and others, telling them that, "We need to leave now." When I awoke, I knew this dream had to do with all of the effort I had been making to get protective masks for my employees and prepare my workplace for the pandemic, as well as convince my family to take protective measures.

Tsunamis, tornados, hurricanes, earthquakes, wildfires, and mass shooters are some of the common metaphors one sees in dreams about any disaster. One dreamer covered much of this list until she made one significant life change:

> I had constant dreams of glowing jellyfish, crumbling and cracking roads that were impossible to get out of without rolling the car, family members lined up on the wharf with a tidal wave coming, flying whales, blimps crashing over the sea, pushing boats across coral & rocks to safety with family and friends in the boat, rollercoasters, hiding & running & packing belongings.....but all catastrophic dreams came to an abrupt halt when I made the decision to leave work and stay home with the virus starting to get out of hand....the VERY first night!!

Metaphoric dreams may also make direct reference to some detail of this pandemic—interspersing the scary visual metaphor with actual guidance. New York's Governor Cuomo tells people they have to shelter in place because of the swarms of bugs or shooters in the streets. President Trump announces there is no tsunami, calling it "fake news." Again our oh-so-visual dreams seem to have produced images worthy of these precautions and debates.

My own dreams in March as the pandemic loomed weren't quite literally about the virus, but of only mildly transformed threats:

> In my first dream, I was in the library of a home that felt centuries old. It was cozy and safe in the among the leather-bound volumes illuminated by a glowing oil lamp, but I knew that outside, a terrible plague was ravaging the world. As the dream continued, I became less able to focus on the library and more overwhelmed by the unseen horror outside. It felt much more like Europe during the Black Plague than modern COVID-19 times.

When I woke up, I made the illustration, "Help, I can't wake up!" featuring a classic European plague doctor walking across a landscape of COVID-19 particles which is on the cover of this book. He's my leading association to plague times. And a very familiar figure: I collect masks, go to masks exhibits, was in Venice last year. I know his mask well, but referred to old lithographs in getting the whole costume accurate.

> In my second dream a few nights later, I was trying to put a hood over my cat Morpheus's head to protect him from toxins in the air. We had to go somewhere outside

through the poisonous air and I was
terrified I wouldn't succeed in protecting
him. He didn't understand that this was
beneficial and he struggled vigorously with
me. Finally, I got the hood on him, picked
him up under my arm, and headed out into
the toxic environment. I think I had a hood
on also. I felt like now we might make it OK.

I think the cat I'm desperate to protect represents my
relative feeling of safety for myself as I finished
teaching my class remotely while my students include
psychiatry residents who were suddenly reassigned to
COVID-19-screenings before good PPE was in place. I
wanted to make an illustration of the dream with a
photocollage which I'd then digitally manipulate to get
the dream's look. I started off looking for pictures of
either a cat in a gas mask or a gas mask the right shape
to superimpose on a photo of Morpheus. However, I
found a person carrying a lamb in just the right posture
with a gas mask over its face. The lamb looks oddly
like my huge whitish cat. Figure 3 is that image, *Strange
Times*.

Figure 3: Strange Times by Deirdre Barrett

Other metaphors are one of a kind, wildly far away from the literal pandemic but also from any common tropes:

> It was a beautiful, sunny day filled with people, and we are sitting and chatting on a bench. Suddenly we hear a noise and we see up in the sky a giant revolver - maybe the size of the zeppelin--flying very fast, changing directions suddenly and targeting people to create a fire explosion and killing them. It aims at us and I start running and try to hide.

> I had a dream that Oprah was trying to kill me and my gang of friends. We escaped her henchmen, but she captured us and sent us to a giant gymnasium filled with hundreds of people, all spread out on mattresses on the floor. Then, Oprah comes to the mic and announces that some of her lucky guests are going to get an amazing "happy ending". She then proceeds to take out a handheld circular saw. I wake up out of terror.

> Dream: I was in Kensington Market (a Bohemian neighborhood in downtown Toronto). A shop that had been shuttered due to the virus had been covertly transformed into a cabaret bar. A singing duo I described as Brechtian (after playwright Bertolt Brecht) went onto the stage to sing one of their songs. The lyrics warning of a coming disaster. Upon waking,

I looked up "Brechtian" and learned of a theatrical concept coined by Brecht, "the distancing effect."

I dreamt that the laws of physics had somehow been repealed. I recall seeing the ocean, only it curled up into the sky and partially overhead, like something out of the movie Inception, only with water instead of buildings. On the other side it was hazy, but you could see the outlines of monsters-- dragons or dinosaurs, moving in the haze or behind it, like a scrim, as if they were getting ready to come into our world. The ground would randomly and occasionally become porous, such that people would suddenly fall into the ground and disappear. In the dream, I recall hearing on the radio (my clock radio may have come on at this point) that this was a new thing and these phenomena were actually occurring. This one, at least, seems to make sense: a natural phenomenon that is (a) new and (b) over which we didn't have any control, but that was harming or ready to harm us.

A final metaphoric dream about the virus provided a companion symbol for a method to deal with it:

I dreamt I was sitting on my couch at home, relaxing at night. This tranquility ended abruptly upon discovering that a rodent had found its way into my home. What alarmed me more is that the rodent was not the scurrying kind, but rather the flying kind. Yes, I dreamt a tiny bat was fluttering within our walls. Though I love animals, I sensed the threat (rabies) this bat could pose to my family, and instinctively went to fight it. Scanning around me, I found a couple newspapers: a thin community newspaper, and a weighty *Washington Post*. I decided to grab the *Post* and swat at the bat, as I would do if a wasp or hornet were buzzing around. After harrowing attempts, in which I could clearly hear the fluttering of the bat's wings and felt waves of cool air, I finally knocked out the bat. Approaching it, it's face was so vivid, and so textured, like nothing I've experienced before in a dream. While not usually one for symbolism, as I woke up panting, it struck me that bats are the likely source of the novel COVID-19 virus. And swatting at this bat, barely visible while flying, with a heavy Washington Post perhaps symbolizes the need to arm oneself with information, data, and knowledge to protect against an invisible virus quickly circulating way too close to home.

Figure 4 is a word cloud created from the first 4,000 dreams submitted to the survey--a visualization of the most frequent words in the survey dreams with common English words omitted (which word-cloud programs do automatically) and also words which are at least half as common in a normative sample of 1,000 previous dreams omitted by hand. Synonyms for anxiety, disease, doctors, and death dominate—with plenty of virus-specific terms.

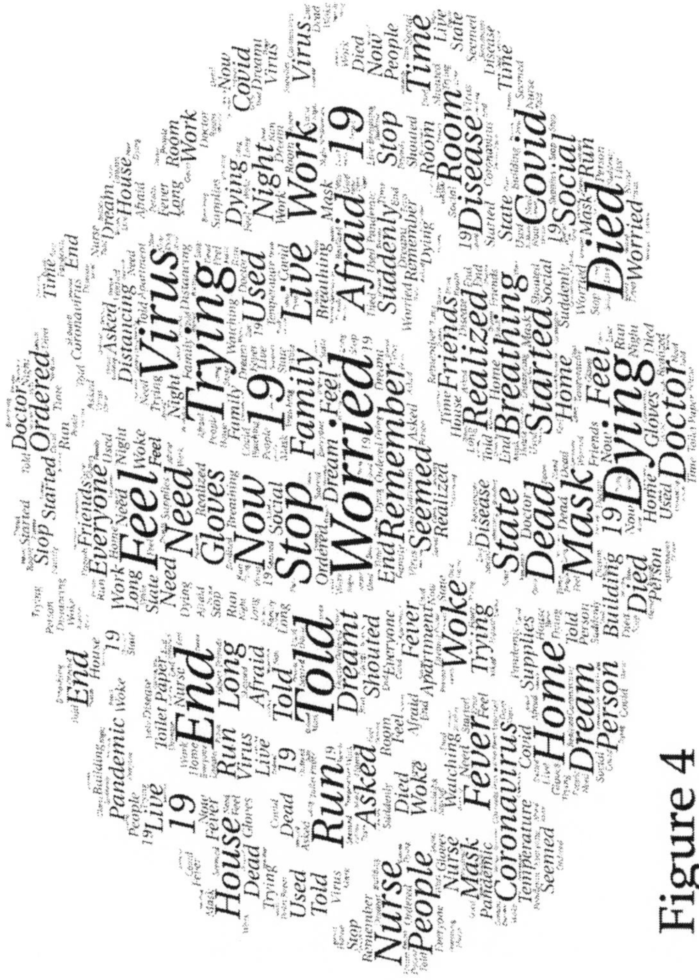

Figure 4

33

Action: Reducing anxiety dreams

> Try to pose for yourself this task: not to
> think of a polar bear, and you will see that
> the cursed thing will come to mind every
> minute.
> >   -Fyodor Dostoevsky, *Winter Notes*
> *on Summer Impressions,*1863

Research on ironic process theory, or "the white bear
problem," confirms that deliberate attempts to muffle
specific thoughts make them more likely to surface, so
it is unproductive to try to suppress anxiety-producing
or depressing topics. If you are disturbed by repetitive
anxiety dreams, you do not want to expend energy
struggling not to have them. The best remedy is to
think of what dreams you would enjoy.

Perhaps there's a loved one you can't be with right
now who you'd like to visit with in your dreams? Or a
favorite vacation spot? Many people enjoy flying
dreams. Maybe you have one all-time favorite dream
you'd like to revisit? With what we call "dream
incubation," borrowed from the term used at the
ancient Greek dream temples, you can suggest to
yourself what you would like to dream as you fall
asleep.

Dreams are extremely visual, so an image is especially
likely to get through to your dreaming mind. Picture
that favorite person, place, or yourself soaring above it
all. Or replay that favorite dream in detailed scenes. If

images don't come easily to you, place a photo or other objects related to the topic on your night table as the last thing to view before turning off the light. Repeat to yourself what you want to dream about as you drift off to sleep.

The technique makes for a pleasant experience as you're falling asleep and greatly raises the odds that your dreaming mind will honor your request.

Chapter 3) Traumatic nightmares

Health care workers

I'm an Italian anesthesiologist. My dream was about an old man, who was suffering from shortness of breath and respiratory failure because of COVID-19. I was the only person in the building able to help him and I had to intubate him. He looked especially challenging in airway anatomy, so I prepared everything ahead. When I was ready to make him fall asleep, I climbed on the bed (something we don't usually do), right back of his head and gave him the drugs to sedate him. As he falls asleep, I lose my balance and tumble out of bed and out of the window next to it, dragging the old man with me from the sixth floor of the building. When I reach the ground, I'm unharmed, whereas the man is dead, beheaded and I feel sad and ashamed.

For context: I work at an incineration plant that receives biohazardous waste including COVI-19. My dream is being on the operations area supervising the maneuvering of taking everything that has to be incinerated and someone drops a barrel that has coveralls and gloves all labeled as "COVID-19+" and for some reason I didn't have my suit nor any PPE and immediately started coughing in my dream. I somehow ended up in an ICU and kept refusing treatment and a doctor friend told me they couldn't allow it and started intubating me. This is when I woke up, nearly time to get up and go to work.

The sample of dreams I collected after 9/11 and this one are similar in that the ordinary person who's watching events on television is stressed and worried about it, but not experiencing what psychologists usually mean by trauma. Typical dreamers are having anxiety dreams, but the majority aren't nightmares. During disasters, however, it is clear who does have terrible nightmares--those who directly experience the horrors. In some traumatized populations, up to 100% of the survivors suffer horrible dreams during or right after the event. Post-traumatic nightmares typically replay terrifying daytime experiences. A NYC policeman dreams of watching the bodies fall from the World Trade Center as he stands helplessly in front of it. A man who worked nearby dreams of "just looking back over my shoulder and seeing the building thundering down."

Horrors only threatened in waking life materialize in dreams. A Kuwaiti woman who watched Iraqi soldiers hold guns to her children's heads, demanding to know where a resistance-fighter cousin is, dreams that they pull the trigger. A worker from a low floor of the World Trade Center dreams of barely escaping as in real life but then seeing--among the dead in the street-- his wife. She actually worked in the building but they'd been safely reunited within the hour.

I'm seeing similar traumatic nightmares in the pandemic survey. Six hundred healthcare workers have responded and many of their dreams re-enact the worst moments of their days. They're trying to intubate a patient whose airway is too constricted. They get a tube into someone and it slips back out. The ventilator malfunctions. Sometimes, there's a dreamlike element as with the Italian doctor falling out of the window with his patient.

The ventilator machines may be old-fashioned ones the nurse has no idea how to operate or they may be replaced by a water cooler just as the doctor is about to attach the tube. Patients that dreamers struggle to save transform into their colleagues, supervisors, or friends. Despite minor variations, the theme is the same: there's a critically ill patient in their care, something is not working, and the patient is dying. They feel desperately responsible and yet have no control over death.

A phenomenon I'm also seeing with the traumatic nightmares of the pandemic are breaches of the physical paralysis people normally have during dreaming: dreamers cry out, or move along with their dreams. Others find them so vivid they are confused about whether they may be real events. All of these are serious but rare sleep disorders that trouble some people over a lifetime, but they can also occur temporarily along with the most intense trauma dreams, which is what seems to be happening now:

> I have been having multiple dreams of
> contracting the Corona virus from work (I

am an ICU nurse) and needing to prove myself due to respiratory failure. In my dreams, I'm always unable to find the correct equipment to appropriately prone myself. My husband reports that I thrash about onto my stomach in the prone position multiple times and am generally restless during sleep since the pandemic began.

I woke up in bed yesterday morning with a start -- at the moment of waking, my arms were actively reaching out to my side to reconnect my patient's ventilator tubing to his endotracheal breathing tube . He had become disconnected. I don't remember the dream itself. This is the only time I remember actually doing an action in real life rather than just dreaming that I did it.

The dreams of are my patients dying. I've been working with critically ill patients in the ICU for the last 7 years, but I have never had dreams about them like this. I woke up sobbing one morning, which I've never done before.

My dreams are all about my work at the hospital. They are so realistic that I often find myself confusing events in my dreams with reality as I am at work throughout the day. There have been so many policy and procedure changes that I have been

confusing the changes in my dreams with
actual policy / procedure changes.

When medical workers dream of their family catching
the virus, it doesn't stop at the realization they could
die as it does for other dreamers. The next step is
usually "and I realize they caught it from me," and the
healthcare provider feels that their loved one "is going
to die because of me."

While the majority of the medical professionals'
dreams are about desperately trying to save patients,
there are some fear-for-oneself dreams as well. These
are more extreme than ordinary people's fear of
catching the virus. The health care workers *know*
they're with highly contagious people and this is
dramatized in nightmares:

> In my most recent dream, the patients had
> to be chained to their beds as the virus made
> them enraged and extremely aggressive. We
> still had to care for them despite them
> struggling to attack us.

> I dreamed that the main point of our
> hospital was to confine patients who were
> zombies who wanted to escape into the
> community and infect others with the
> zombie virus. We were racing around
> making sure all wards were locked and that
> windows were latched. But then a few
> "patients" escaped the hospital and made it
> into the community. I knew that we had

failed and the whole city would die because we didn't contain them.

"Survivor guilt" is a popular term in the literature of trauma. Some people indeed irrationally feel they don't deserve to live if others died. But many dream examples from traumas seem more to express the idea that, "There but for the grace of God, go I," or echo superstitions that one can only cheat death briefly. One woman, whose house narrowly escaped destruction in Berkeley's 1991 firestorm, dreamed, "The fire had developed an organismic consciousness. . . It waited for fire departments to leave and came back to get the houses it had missed." A vet who in waking life had been called upon to identify a friend killed in a battle, in his recurring dream unzips the same green body bag--*and the dead face revealed is his own.*

I am seeing these dreams of guilt and vicarious reenactments in the pandemic healthcare workers:

> I have an expired medical license that is not renewable without some updates to my training, so I have a lot of guilt. My younger brother is a physician in a high risk setting. I dreamed a hospital contacted me and asked if I would be interested in a job if it were safe. I lied and said I would come to the interview so my brother could come instead and maybe have better working conditions. Once all three of us were there, I came clean. The hospital asked my brother just one question: whether he had been in some room with a weird code-name. My brother

said no and was not offered the job. I asked what the name meant and he said the interviewer was asking if he had been in the room with all of the bodies yet.

I am, in real life, a semi-retired RN, and have worked with critically ill patients until recently, including those on a ventilator . I was a new nurse at the beginning of the AIDS epidemic in 1980, and worked in an urgent care when SARS broke out. I dream am working in an ICU with COVID patients, and they are all dying in spite of our best efforts to save them. I am wearing full isolation gear, as I have in real life in previous work situations. At the end of the dream, I have COVID-19, and feel full of fear. In real life, should I contract it, I am in a vulnerable population.

Another group of people who often have traumatic nightmares when a crisis arises are those who have survived a trauma in the past. They do not have to be directly involved in the new disaster for it to activate PTSD from the previous psychic wound. Some dream mainly of the past event, others of the current one— and hybrid trauma nightmares are common. After 9/11, a middle-aged woman had nightmares about being on planes seized by hijackers—but the man who raped her in her twenties was always one of them. A woman whose mother had severely abused her in childhood dreamed that her mother was back from the dead and co-operating with bin Laden's network. I'm seeing similar reactivation of old traumas in the pandemic dream survey.

I grew up during the Argentinean military dictatorship of the 70s and 80s; terrifying, defining memories persist, and have affected my dreams over the years. I was also a victim of serious domestic violence as a child; and, later in life, I was a volunteer at Ground Zero in the aftermath of 9/11. I mention these things because many of my exhausting, anguished dreams now are variations on these themes. The current epidemic has not inspired as many new dreams as it has added a twist to these recursive narratives. I have always dreamed of my friends and family dying and I have woken up crying, lately it is clear they die of COVID-19. In the aftermath of 9/11, I had nightmares with very specific scenes, (too ugly to recount), involving a baby stroller and some orange body bags I interacted with in actual life. Now somehow my 9/11 dreams, which had decreased after so many years, have come back, entwined with the COVID-19 concerns.

I'm a Vietnam veteran served there in 1968-69 as an infantry soldier and I do have PTSD mainly dealing with survivor guilt. A few weeks ago I had a horrible dream relating to the pandemic and Vietnam. My dream was I was in Vietnam and I got captured by the Viet Cong. After being in captivity a short while, they held me down and they began to inject me with the COVID virus. It was awful. It happened about 4 am and I got out of bed and feeling around for my window and finally found a light to put on and then realized I was safe and at home. Been years since I had any kind of a dream like that.

As a teenager I was locked up in a psychiatric facility in Utah to cure me of being gay. We were treated very badly-- basically abused in an attempt to force us to change. I keep having dreams that I'm back in Utah, in the facility. I am being escorted/carried by the arms and forced down the hallway in the facility. The psych techs who are carrying me/walking me are both wearing COVID-19 style masks. I'm in a hospital gown and I feel exposed and vulnerable. In this dream, I feel like things are out of control and that I'm 15 again, with no hope of a future.

I had a nightmare where I couldn't breathe well and someone was standing at the head of my bed holding a fist over my face. I was paralyzed and could not scream even though I felt my mouth was being held open. My biggest fear is being intubated and on a ventilator again. I have been on one before for my asthma. This dream was about that happening again.

Fever dreams

What I remember about my first dream is having my lungs removed and what looked like lungs for a robot put in. They were on the outside of my body but stuck into the space where my lungs were. The robot lungs were shiny and full of small parts like the motherboard of a computer. They were heavy and made it hard to breathe. I remember looking down at them and holding my chest.

I was feeling so weak and sick. I fell asleep and I felt that I woke up and was thirsty. I walked from my bedroom to the kitchen and after drinking some water, I heard someone scream in my ear! I was so startled and looked up to see a glowing fuzzy ball-like shape that was purplish-blue . It just floated there until, all of a sudden, it flew right past me leaving sparkling dust behind! I swear that this really happened but I know it sound crazy. I was still so shaken when I told my family the next morning. I can still hear that scream in my ears!

Dreams during a high fever are a thing unto themselves—standing out as most bizarre even in an already unusually vivid collection. Physiologically, the dreamer exhibits partly the brain characteristics of sleep, partly those of waking, and partly ones abnormal for any state. They feel and hear some real stimuli, generally wildly misinterpreted. One moment, they know they're in a hospital room, the next they see the interior of a spaceship. Fever dreams are almost always extremely disturbing even though the imagery may not be stereotypically nightmarish. Being in one setting and then another without transition is just shrugged off in an ordinary dream. In the fever dream, however, the dreamer desperately fights to make sense of it—but knows it doesn't make sense. They're hallucinating some elements and perceiving others but can't sort out which is which. I can't tell if the dreamer with the purple-blue ball was wandering around her hall in dream-like hallucinatory state or sound asleep in bed for the whole experience. Either could easily be remembered as the above experience when one has a high fever.

COVID-19 patient Peter Fisk had an assortment of fever dreams during a six day period where he was at home ill and running a fever of 103. He slept much of the time but would rouse to fix occasional meals.

> One day, after sleeping for hours and hours, I got up and I thought, oh, I am going to have some of that smoked fish that I bought and I could visualize it on the shelves where I had put it. So I come into the kitchen to the cupboard and there was nothing there. I was completely puzzled but then I realized--oh that's right, I haven't been shopping for two weeks because I've been sick. I dreamt that.

A stranger yet experience happened when he felt wide awake, but as I've said most of these are probably in an abnormal hybrid state:

I was curled up under lots of covers, and
started thinking how this reminded me of
when I was younger and used to burrow
into river banks and curl up in a nice, cozy,
earthen den. I was remembering how
pleasant it used to be to do that, and why
don't I ever do that anymore?" But then it
occurred to me that I had never actually
done that. I was having false memories of
being an otter.

In his feverish state, Peter also continued to check
websites related to his genealogy hobby. He found that
an unrelated woman he'd never heard of had just
posted a photo of his grandfather, Larry Fisk, as a
young man on the site findagrave.com. He messaged
her, thanking her for posting, forgot about it, and went
back to sleep. The next day, he was puzzled to see a
message from a stranger saying she'd bought a
postcard in an antique shop that had his grandfather's
image on one side and a note from his great-
grandmother on the other describing Larry's bout with
the Spanish Flu in 1918. She offered to mail it to Peter.
He gradually began to hazily recall seeing the image
the previous day so he wrote back with his address—
and went back to sleep.
An imminent postcard from his great-grandmother
describing his grandfather going through a version of
his current ordeal sounded more dreamlike and
unlikely than smoked fish in his kitchen. So, for a few
days after, he thought he'd dreamed this also. But the
postcard arrived. A mostly-recovered Peter has the
card about Larry Fisk, reading in part, "I suppose you

know that he was very sick with flu last fall. We thought we would never see him alive again but God spared his life." Alas, there are no 1918 fever dream accounts on it.

The most famous example of COVID-19 fever dreams so far are those CNN's Chris Cuomo told his brother, New York Gov. Andrew Cuomo during one of the latter's COVID-19 briefings. Chris described "scary" dreams—but again not ones with obviously negative content. "I tell you, Pop (former Gov. Mario Cuomo, who died in 2015) was talking to me," he recounted, "I was seeing people from college--people I haven't seen in forever. It was freaky what happened last night."

And most "freaky": "You came to me in a dream," Chris told Andrew, "You had on a very interesting ballet outfit, and you were dancing in the dream. You were waving a wand, saying 'I wish my wand could make this go away.' And then you spun around and you danced away."

Action: Mastery Dreams and Re-scripting traumatic nightmares

Dulles air traffic controller Danielle O'Brien guided the routine takeoff of American flight 77 on the fateful morning. An hour later she watched it--as a blip on her radar screen—speed toward the White House, veer, and slam into the Pentagon. In the nights that followed, O'Brien had nightmares. "I've sat up straight in bed many times, reliving it, re-seeing it, re-hearing it," she told a reporter. But then, in the magic language only dreams speak, O'Brien dreamed of

> . . . a green pool in front of me that was
> part of the radar scope. It was a pool of
> gel and I reached into the radar scope to
> stop that flight. But in the dream, I didn't
> harm the plane. I just held it in my hand,
> and somehow that stopped everything.

Clinicians--including myself--working with trauma survivors, noticed that a nightmare would occasionally transform into a mastery dream. Dreamers would fight off the rapist, firemen would arrive to extinguish a fire, or magically they'd realize they could just fly away from the battle to a safe place. Two survivors in my 9/11 dream sample found the doomed World Trade Center occupants jumping out of windows the most horrifying image. This replayed in their nightmares— sometimes watching, other times forced to jump themselves. After many repetitions, however, they began to equip themselves and other jumpers with— in one case, parachutes and more fancifully, umbrellas. Dreamers awaken from mastery dreams as comforted by them as they had been re-traumatized by their previous nightmares. Usually the nightmares do not reoccur. Those of us who did group work with trauma survivors further noticed that, if someone in a group discussion of nightmares told an anecdote of "I used to have recurring nightmares, but then one night I dreamed .. .," another member of the group might come back the next week and report a mastery dream. Just hearing that they were possible hastened and boosted their occurrence.

In my 1996 edited book, *Trauma and Dreams*, I gathered chapter authors who'd each arrived at the same idea: that therapists might help these healing dreams to happen more quickly and reliably. They described versions they'd developed to assist survivors in creating a script for a dream which mastered the event in the recurring nightmare. All of the variations involved telling the survivors about mastery dreams. Therapists then asked them if they have an ending they'd like the nightmare to take. Some survivors immediately know what theirs would be. If not, we offer a wide variety of examples: one might have someone rescue you, one might fight off the attacker oneself. The alternate ending could be a realistic or fantastic one where the attacker or natural disaster is shrunk down to microscopic size or shot off into space. Many survivors of childhood sexual abuse choose to make their abuser listen to the dreamer describe on how wrong their acts were as their satisfying conclusion. Whatever ending is chosen, therapists coach their survivors to elaborate visual images and other details and to rehearse these in therapy sessions and/or at bedtime. As survivors fall asleep at night, they can remind themselves, "Tonight if I have the dream of (the fire, Vietnam, etc.), I want to (find a fire hose, freeze the action and speak to the Vietnamese boy . . .) Some resulting dreams are of transcendent dialogues with those one has been brutalized by—or brutalized—but even simply revenge or escape can serve to release the dreamer from a cycle of helpless, trapped repetitions. Just as repetitive nightmares make people more fearful by day, mastery dreams carry over into a sense of strength or comfort.

Sleep physician Barry Krakow consolidated these techniques into a three session group treatment which he and his research team conducted first for groups of rape survivors and later for Vietnam Veterans and other traumatized populations. Their research found that incubating mastery dreams significantly reduced the occurrence of nightmares. The nightmare intervention also improved other post-traumatic stress disorder symptoms, such as daytime anxiety and flashbacks, which had not been addressed directly in the group sessions.

PTSD sufferers can try this on their own but it's most effective if done with a therapist. Trauma therapists are often trained in the technique. After the pandemic ends, many of the healthcare workers dreaming repetitive nightmares will spontaneously stop experiencing them over days to weeks. But for others, the nightmares will linger and they would benefit from this therapy.

Chapter 4) Indirect effects of the pandemic on dreams

Staying at home

> I dreamed I was put in prison—solitary confinement. When I would hear guards outside my door, I would ask what I'd done and when I would be released but no one ever answered.

> All my friends have been exiled to some far-away place. I was in my old haunts but they were completely empty of people.

> I woke up (not for real) and found my apartment filled with everyone from the neighborhood (in reality my in-laws are living with us for the pandemic). People had camp stoves going in corners, cots all through each room and I couldn't find a place to walk or sit.

As the lock-down/stay-at-home/shelter-in-place/quarantine orders have continued, there have been an increase in dreams which focus on this rather than the virus itself. Those who are home alone dream scenarios that exaggerate their loneliness: they're in all sorts of prisons, or the person I quoted in the introduction to the book got stranded alone on Saturn and another woman had a very similar dream in which she'd been selected to be the first colonist on Mars—a job she

had *not* applied for. Some people dream of going
on their daily walks and finding the streets are
suddenly deserted. One dreamed her dog
vanished from her apartment.

At the other end of the spectrum, people are
sheltering with their families and sometimes with
even more extended family than those with
whom they usually reside. They dream of their
house being converted into a homeless shelter, a
testing site, or neighbors barge in and "borrow"
all their toilet paper. One woman who is finding
her boyfriend is a handful because of his
immaturity dreams that he turns into an actual
child who runs outside for ice-cream and she
must chase him down.

There are a smaller set of happy dreams that dramatize
positive feelings about lockdown. An introvert dreams
of feeling safe in a little tower. A mother dreams of
playing with her children and husband in their house.

And there are wish-fulfillment dreams about events
not resembling the dreamers' real quarantine
situations. I saw a lot of these in the 500 dreams from
the WWII POW's. For the soldiers, there were dreams
of being back at the family home or visits to favorite
pubs with friends—often combined with more favorite
foods than I've seen in any other set of dreams:

> I was at home and went to the larder and ate
> everything I could see. Went out and met
> my sister and a friend at a restaurant and
> had a large dinner. Then went to another

pub and had some food there. Then went to
another pub and had more food. West back
to the first pub and found a good mixture of
drinks-- barley wine and mild ale. Then I
had a dish of prunes and custard into which
a bottle of ale had also been poured. I
rejoined my sister and had another meal.
Then back to the pub and had a large
mixture of various snacks.

Pandemic wish-fulfillment dreams occasionally feature
favorite foods, but more often favorite people and
settings:

Birthday party with animatronic animals in
the water dressed up in costumes. Kinda
like Aladdin but the animals were jungle
animals. The party had a lot going on and I
was shouting for everyone to bring swim
suits. (I think I had this dream 'cause my
bestie's Zoom party is today and I'm
missing doing stuff like that at Disneyland
since the animals were reminiscent of their
jungle cruise).

Those at Camp-Home-Alone may dream of sheltering
with a friend or lover. Others who are crowded in with
family or roommates discover their house has a secret
room no one else knows about that they can retreat to.
Some are sheltering with old flames—to romantic or
toxic effect. One woman is back with an old boyfriend
who is professing that he should never have left.
Another is housed with a former partner who spends
the quarantine criticizing her for letting her leg hair

grow. And the pandemic period has spawned new fantasies:

> I dreamt that Gov. Cuomo and I were involved in an illicit affair. We were in a fancy high rise and rode down in an elevator together and thru a set of security turnstiles (like the subway) and parted. I felt a tremendous sense of abandonment and said to myself, "but I don't have keys." I spent the rest of the dream in squalid areas of the building - a windowless bedroom, a ground floor public restroom where loud and vulgar people were wearing masks, but not in the right way. I kept trying to get back upstairs--the safe place was in Cuomo's affection and apartment.

Masks, homeschooling, work, and finances

> The masks on people's faces had fused into place so you couldn't take them off and I was never able to see anyone's full face again.

Masks, which featured early on as protection that dreamers panicked when they discovered they or others lacked, gradually are portrayed more often as a lonely barrier similar to dreams about isolating at home. Dreamers can't eat because of masks, are trying to speak but can't be heard because of them, or are suffocated by masks they can't remove. Homeschooling and job situations are similarly increasing as disturbing dream themes:

> I am currently living with a family that I nanny for and so I am working every day homeschooling the kids and every night I'll have a dream where I'm still teaching and it's never ending. I've also had a lot of dreams where the parents tell me that they got laid off of work and I no longer have a job

> I am homeschooling my ten-year-old. I dreamed that the school contacted me to say it had been decided that his whole class would come to my home and I was supposed to teach all of them for however long the school remained closed.

Parents and childcare workers who have not been trained as teachers dream exaggerated versions of the challenges of homeschooling. Or of their role continuing: the pandemic is over and their city has decided not to reopen schools but rather to have all children educated by parents until age 18. One mother has to take her child's math exam and her child is failing because of her score.

People who are stressed by being required to go to a job they view as risky dream of walking on filthy carpet or sharing a cubicle with a coughing co-worker. Those who are furloughed dream this is extended for five years . . . or that they are fired for good. One man worried about his dwindling finances dreams of grocery shopping; when he goes to check out, he opens his wallet and it is emptied of money. Then he remembers his credit card has been confiscated also.

Reopening

While there were a few early dreams depicting pleasure that everything had returned to normal, those were usually cast as "The pandemic is somehow over . . ." or "There must be a cure or something 'cause everyone is able to be out without masks." Dreams explicitly about reopening before there's a cure have increased as cities, states and countries do so. They are almost all fearful. Many are simply dramatizations of what could happen:

> I work at a restaurant that was drive-thru only for more than a month and when I found out we were going to take dine-ins again, I had a dream where we reopened our buffet and people packed into the restaurant like sardines in a can. They were angry and getting close to my face to shout. The buffet and salad bar were a mess. Half the people were coughing and looked like death. We were so packed that a kid got trampled and his arm was broken. I was horrified.

> During the first 5 to 6 weeks, in all my dreams, something terrible was happening to my husband, myself, and our teenage daughter. We were trapped, or held against our will. In others, we were very ill and

there were no drugs left for us, or no doctors available. Then I adjusted and the bad dreams went away. Now that our city is opening up again--restaurants are fully open for indoor service, and with the recent gatherings for protests--the dreams are intense and scary again: I'm getting sick, in the ICU, and not surviving. I wake up with my jaws clenched and a terrible headache.

Others have more bizarre depictions of inappropriate reopening:

I dreamed our town had reopened, and so me and some friends went out to watch a parade. It was really festive with music, balloons and food stands. Every so often, medics would push their way through the crowd and come out carrying a stretcher with a corpse. The parade continued but more and more people died and were carried away.

There was a new law that prohibited regulations that would have restricted any religious activities. Movie theaters used that as a loophole to reopen to show religious movies. I found myself in a committee discussing whether movies were Christian or not. One controversial subject was, if James Bond could be seen as a Christ-like figure and "No Time to Die" should be allowed to be shown.

Action: Incubating problem-solving dreams

If you are interested in steering your dreams toward potentially solving some of these problems rather than simply dramatizing them, "dream incubation" is a technique for influencing our dreams. In one study that I did, college students incubated solutions to objective problems of their own choosing that they actually had to solve but could put aside waking efforts on for one week. I specified only that the problem must matter to them and that it have a recognizable solution.

Each night for a week, students incubated a dream on their problem. They recorded their dreams and noted ones they thought addressed the problem or contained a satisfactory solution. Two raters also judged whether the dreams focused on the problems--or solved them.

My subjects chose a range of issues: academic, medical, and personal. Whether because of the modest level of difficulty or the relevance to students' lives, half of my students had dreams they felt addressed their problem. One-third dreamed a solution to it. The judges, who didn't know which dream went with which problem, rated the same half as addressing the problem and only slightly fewer dreams—1/4--as solving them. Many successful dreams concerned major life decisions. The following example was rated as solved by both the dreamer and the judges:

> Problem: I have applied to two clinical psychology programs and two in industrial psychology because I just can't decide which field I want to go into.

<u>Dream</u>: A map of the United States. I'm in a plane flying over this map. The pilot says we're having engine trouble and need to land. We look for a safe place on the map indicated by a light. I ask about Massachusetts which we're right over, but he says that all of Massachusetts is very dangerous. The lights seemed to be further west.

<u>Solution</u>: I woke up and realized that my two clinical schools are both in Massachusetts where I've spent my whole life and where my parents live. Both industrial programs are far away, Texas and California. This is because originally I was looking to stay close to home and there were no good industrial programs nearby. I realized that there is a lot wrong with staying at home and, funny as it sounds, getting away is probably more important than which kind of program I go into.

You might like to incubate a dream about something objective like, "How could we re-arrange the furniture to give everyone more privacy?" or "What could I do to earn money while I'm furloughed from my regular job?" Or perhaps an emotional issue such as "What can I do differently to stop these constant petty quarrels with my husband?" or "How do I stop worrying about aspects of this crisis which I can't control?" For any of these, try the incubation instructions that were successful in my research:

1) Write down the problem as a brief phrase or sentence and place this by the bed.

2) Review the problem for a few minutes just before going to bed.

3) Once in bed, visualize the problem as a concrete image if it lends itself to this.

4) Tell yourself you want to dream about the problem just as you are drifting off to sleep.

5) Keep a pen and paper—or your smart phone--on the night table.

6) Upon awakening, lie quietly before getting out of bed. Note whether there is any trace of a recalled dream and invite more of the dream to return if possible. Write it down.

Optional steps to increase efficacy also include:

7) At bedtime, visualize yourself dreaming about the problem, awakening, and writing on the bedside note pad.

8) Arrange objects connected to the problem on the night table or on the wall across from bed if they lend themselves to a poster.

Chapter 5) How will our world change?

Post-apocalyptic scenarios

People had evolved to have 12-foot radius invisible bubbles that acted like forcefields and we weren't able to touch another person again until the human race died off. Most of my COVID dreams take place in the future after society has collapsed and everyone is living in some sort of futuristic wild west. Last night I dreamt I was in a small community of COVID-free people in some far northern latitude that existed in polar night. I was out skiing (I've never touched a ski) and came across an aggressive polar bear I had to shoot (I've never touched a gun).

I dreamed that I worked in a factory in a post-apocalyptic future, forced to wear an old fashioned plague doctor mask. It felt very real, and I woke up with my heart racing.

I dream about isolation, not having children, and themes that revolve around a bleak future, or one for which I am unprepared.

I dreamed of never returning to life-as-normal, of being old and quarantined with my future grandchildren.

As the pandemic drags on, more dreams come into the survey that envision our future. Some are set in a dark one. For one dreamer, the virus has turned everyone except his family into zombies who they must constantly evade. Others see a small, ravaged population of survivors with few resources, like the fictional world of *Pandemic*. A few meet violent lawless gangs in a landscape resembling *Mad Max*.

Yet another group of dreams foretell the world's end from the vantage point of our current time:

> The only COVID-19-related dream I had involved being interviewed by the local news because the Pope had confided in me that the world was ending in July of this year, related to the virus and other factors. The local news set up a camera in my living room and was asking me questions about my conversation with the Pope and how the world would end.

> Dreamt that I realized the Mayans predicted the apocalypse for 2020. I had a sense of extreme sadness and dread because I knew COVID was the beginning of the end. I knew that the world must end at the conclusion of 2020. I didn't want to tell my mother, because that is such sad news -- that we will all die soon. I was shocked that I was the first one to make this connection and remember the Mayan prediction for 2020. I wanted to tweet about it because I

thought people would agree that COVID
must be a sign of the end.

One woman experienced herself as among last entities
in existence:

> I dreamt that all of humanity was slowly
> blinking out of existence, preserved only by
> me forcefully willing everyone to stay by
> remembering them.

Another had a symmetrical scenario—it was she who
was disappearing:

> I had a dream that the world was ending.
> This dream did not feel like a dream but
> rather the future. It was too clear to be a
> dream. It was like particles of matter were
> being removed from my body as they
> removed the universe.

Dreaming the cure

There are a smaller set of highly optimistic dreams that
the dreamer or others discovered a cure for COVID-19:

> In my dream it was found that leeches were
> a cure for COVID-19, and as many leeches
> as possible were gathered to help those who
> had tested positive for the virus.

> I was sitting and discussing how good the
> medical community was that was able to
> solve the corona crisis. They had found out

that microwaves were able to block the virus from reproducing. If you got the virus, you were moved to big community halls where there were transmitters sending out microwaves. Like the ones in the microwave ovens, but not as powerful. After staying in the hall for 1 to 6 weeks most patients were able to create enough antibodies to defeat the virus, reducing the death toll to almost zero.

Dreamt that I found the cure for the virus. Had to do with the saliva of housecats. Woke up before I could remember any details as to how the discovery was made and if it worked.

I dreamt that SARS-cov 2, as proteins, make music and so, to find the cure, scientists had to compose a melody that fit with the one SARS-cov 2 produced. Then they injected this as a vaccine and people get well.

Most of the dreams of curative techniques in my sample don't sound especially likely. Cats do get infected with the virus without getting very sick, so *possibly* the immunoglobulin-A in their saliva is better protection than ours. *Lots* of leeches probably lowered blood pressure a bit in olden times and they're still used in a few specialized settings for the blood-thinning peptides they inject into patients . . . but they don't suck viruses out. And the injectable music one is . . . mostly delightful. See Figure 5 for an even more

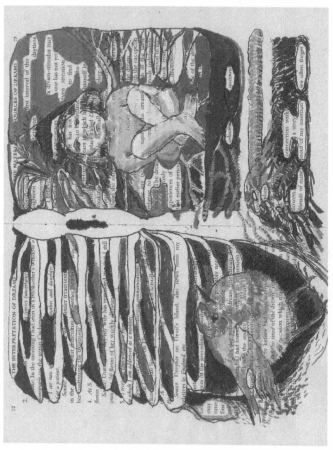

Figure 5: Julia Lockheart's painting of Chloe Douglas's dream during Mark Blagrove's Ullman-style dreamwork on DreamsID.

66

fanciful cure in which a friendly robin plucks all of the COVID-19 particles out of a dreamer's lungs.

Some dreamed cures are plausibly related to medical science:

> I dreamed there will be a substance either inhaled or nose spray that will coat the mucosal cells with something that will block and or neutralize the virus and prevent it from entering cells. Not a vaccine. The technology would be developed separately for all classes of viruses and also lead to a "cure" for the common cold. It involved introducing an antibody or something else in the spray.

> My dream said there would be a "piggybacking" virus that will attach to COVID-19 and neutralize it. I am a psychologist and never heard of anything like a "piggy backing" virus but after the dream looked it up and it is a real thing and there is one being used for SARS-COV. I had no idea this even existed until after the dream.

Andy Sarjahani, the young man with the *Home Alone* cardboard cutouts dream, dreamed up a diagnostic procedure rather than a cure:

> I was with my dog June at the neighborhood grocery store. She was on a leash—strange,

but then I realized dogs were allowed in stores now. We were in the produce section. I was trying to get through as soon as possible. June would periodically tug at my pants leg to pull me away from someone. I realized she could smell who had the virus and was protecting me.

Ten days after this dream, Andy saw the first article about research training dogs to detect asymptomatic infections. He remembered reading years before that specially trained dogs had great accuracy with sniffing out cancer. There are now several research groups on both sides of the Atlantic exploring dogs as detectors for public settings such as airports.

Neither the sniffing dogs nor piggyback viruses were discovered because of the recent dreams. Some medical and scientific discoveries, however, have come in dreams. Canadian physician Frederick Banting was knighted for developing a method of isolating the hormone insulin after seeing the technique in a dream. August Kekulé dreamed the molecular structure of benzene. Otto Loewi received the Nobel Prize in Physiology or Medicine for an experiment demonstrating the chemical nature of nerve conduction, which he performed exactly as he had dreamed. So we should pay attention to dream cures-- especially if dreamed by people with backgrounds in medicine and biology.

Other optimistic dreams

Positive dreams can be totally unrealistic but

nevertheless serve to improve the dreamer's mood or outlook:

> A tsunami was approaching, I live in Michigan, and I had been training to go out onto the wave and save people.

> I got on a rollercoaster and it went slowly, very, very high and literally just stayed upside down for seemingly hours. But I felt fine, because I thought I'm not afraid of heights and I'm not getting motion sickness. I needed to tell myself I was OK to keep calm. (like now during the COVID-19 pandemic)

Christians who dream religious themes don't always visit an old testament apocalypse, but rather some dream of a positive second coming:

> I had a dream last night that this is the time that Jesus is returning. It was so surreal and we were all preparing to be gone soon since he would be calling us home.

Atheists can also have Christian themes bubble up from childhood:

> I dreamed I went to my doctor for a routine visit and, totally unexpectedly, he diagnosed me with COVID-19. I was so shocked that I ran out of his office, only realizing later that I had not taken the prescription for meds that could save my

life. By then I was 30 miles away so I went to a Christian-based clinic where they also diagnosed me as having COVID-19, but told me that the only way I could be cured was to accept Jesus into my life.

That's the dream. I am an atheist for the record, and teach evolutionary biology at a college, so I am often teaching about evolution vs. creationism. Also, my dad was a minister. Have fun with that one!

Other dreams reference positive signs from other religious traditions:

The white buffalo calf named Miracle came to me, or I was there by her. She lived 1994-2004 in Janesville WI, a couple hours south of me. Her birth was a prophetic sign for the Lakota, uniting the different races of man, dramatic earth changes but meant to be a good omen.

The planet heals

There are visions of positive changes for the earth, such as to the environment:

I was in my living room when an object appeared above our neighborhood--a large spacecraft, dark metallic and octagonal in shape, descending toward our street. I went out onto our deck and could hear the neighbors yelling and screaming 'oh my god! aliens are landing!', but I felt calm. I knew it was coming to us from the future, and was piloted by humans with good intentions. When they landed, a few disembarked with leaflets in their hands. One of them climbed the stairs to our deck with a sincere, serious expression on his face. He told me they were here to warn us that we needed to take this virus seriously, and welcome it as a teacher. We were killing the planet and the ecosystem we need to survive as humans. They were here to spread the word but they couldn't stay long as they would attract violence to themselves. I confirmed there were three people in my neighborhood with weapons pointed at them right now, and they were looking to me for any signal of distress. So I smiled and made a gesture of thanks (hands together at my heart, as in 'namaste'), and told them to go and save themselves. We would get the word out.

Others glimpse a future with whales or dolphins frolicking at the shore because of human absence. More bizarrely, one dreamer emerged from quarantine to find the whales had learned to fly. Some found cleaner water in their cities' rivers and lakes. One dreamer was in her back yard which appeared as usual except that large mountain peaks rose up in the distance; her mother told her that pollution had hidden these for decades.

Sometimes the theme of fixing our planet's environment and even the intent of deities, as in the following, seemed at odds with human survival:

> I dreamt that I was booking a trip to California for me and my family, from the East Coast where we live. I was happy because it was possible again, the Coronavirus had died down mostly. Not completely. However, a new and even worse virus just then started popping up in California. I realized then that the world's population was going to be decimated. At least half the people in the world were going to die. I was struck by how it seemed that nature had enough of humans and was taking care of the planet by getting rid of us. At the same time it felt like some type of force, I don't believe in god, but something like a god was sinisterly doing all this.

> I had a dream I was trying to talk to Mother Nature about the covid crisis. She was in the form of Gaia and eating peaches from a peach tree. She seemed indifferent to my asking to help out humanity. She nodded and said maybe with a coy smile. I then woke up.

One scenario featured hope, disaster, and then hope for different solution:

> There was a world crisis where as many humans as possible were attempting to leave our planet. People were boarding any

ship they could - tiny house boats to gigantic cruise ships. We were floating in a giant convoy - picking up new passengers and ships as we were preparing to leave. I was flying around (some folks had developed this superpower), taking last looks of the Earth and trying to convince people to go. I was involved with the government, somehow. There were stragglers - folks who couldn't or wouldn't board the ships. Those poor souls, I thought to myself. There was so much hope in the convoy. All of the ships began an assent - rising out of the ocean and then angling towards the heavens. It was a sight to behold - seeing the hope for humanity's future, ready to continue the species as explorers and settlers of new worlds. We escaped the atmosphere and entered space - and then - an epic fail. Not a single ship had atmosphere containment. People instantly suffocated - millions of bodies just poured out of these ships, in the most tragic of leadership/governmental failures. So much loss - from such tragic incompetency. I held my breath and flew back down to Earth, feeling crushing shock and disbelief. My flight abilities were failing - a sign of the weight of the tragedy. The stragglers and non-conformists, it turned out, were the true carriers of Earth's human legacy. The President had been duplicitous and although he said he was going to leave Earth in the convoy had decided to stay behind. I wondered how Earth's people could stomach to have such a leader in place. The dream ended with a glimmer of hope - the next great human mission was going to be an all-out attempt to save the planet, instead of fleeing it.

One woman dreamed with whimsical optimism of a plan for economic recovery:

> I recently had a dream that Bernie Sanders was president because Trump and Biden died from COVID-19. Sanders came on TV and was asking all of us to become drug dealers and told us to start growing pot plants in our back yards — but no more than five. He was teaching us how to germinate the seeds. He said this would boost the economy.

Action: Cultivating big dreams

Most of the handful of optimistic dreams so far in my survey mostly cheer up the dreamer . . . which is not a small thing, but I expect to see more dreams imagining the future—personal and global--as the pandemic wears on. Crises can be a time when one sees what Carl Jung referred to as "Big Dreams," which he observed "are often remembered for a lifetime" and may "prove to be the richest jewel in the treasure-house of psychic experience." I've known people who have chosen their vocation or their spouse based on a transcendent dream—or who have stepped away from ordinary pursuits to devote themselves to a larger cause for their lifetime because of dreaming a new path. Big dreams have changed the world: Mahatma Gandhi, despondent at the British-controlled parliament's rejection of India's proposal for greater independence, dreamed of calling for strikes of non-violent disruption of the country's business and social systems—which eventually brought about *total* independence.

The dream incubation techniques at the end of Chapter 4 can also be applied to these larger issues. You might consider incubating a dream of:

A way you can be part of the solution to our current crisis

The life you wish to live after the pandemic end

The future of our planet . . . and your role in it

Conclusion

We've seen how dreaming reflected each aspect of the pandemic: fear of catching the virus, reactions to sheltering at home, work changes, homeschooling, and an individual's increased isolation or crowding. Some patterns proved quite similar to those seen in dreams during other crises: front-line health care workers are tormented by nightmares reenacting daytime traumas, while the general population experienced more anxiety dreams but also a range from bizarre nightmares to positive inspirational dreams. The metaphors that have been distinctive during the COVID-19 threat are the bug-attacks and the invisible monsters: these reflect that this threat is less concrete than others we have faced.

Over the past three months, dreams have progressed from fear of the mysterious new threat . . . to impatience with restrictions . . . to more fear again as the world begins to reopen. And dreams have just begun to consider the big picture: how society may change. The progression of pandemic dreams is not over and my survey continues. If you too are having dreams about this unprecedented time, I invite you to submit them at
https://www.surveymonkey.com/r/B8S75CN.

This short book arrives early in the epoch which the broader survey will document more fully. Much of the world, however, is in a crucial transition from total lock-down to gradual reopening. We are searching for the level of precautions that will allow more usual pursuits to exist alongside the continuing threat of the virus. Now is a meaningful time to take note of what dreams have reflected during this first phase of the pandemic. I also wanted to catch this moment when so many people are paying heightened attention to their dreams. Many of you have experienced fascinating metaphors and have watched your sleeping mind processing waking concerns in creative ways. You may have had a dream that helped you understand anxieties or move past them or one that offered wise counsel on dealing with the pandemic. Dreams operate in this manner by their nature, but you can optimize what you gain from them by the techniques described in this book: dream journaling, interpretation, redirecting repetitive anxiety dreams, and incubating dreams for help with the topics or problems that most concern you. I hope that people will not leave their new-found interest in the dreamworld behind as we return to external pursuits, but will carry it forward into this brave new world.

Acknowledgements

I would like to thank Nancy Grace, Ruth Lingford, and Stuart Krichevsky for comments which enhanced the book's content and readability. I'm grateful to psychologist Mark Blagrove and artist Julia Lockheart of DreamsID, and dreamers Mia Muliau and Chloe Douglas, for allowing me to use Julia's drawings and the dream accounts from Mia and Chloe that were featured in Mark and Julia's fascinating FaceBook dreamwork groups. I appreciate permission from TIME Magazine to use the still of Andy Sarjahani's dream from the upcoming short film produced by Kathleen Flynn and Margaret Cheatham Williams and animated by Maya Edelman; keep an eye out for that appearing on Time.com. An excellent article by Craig Semon in the Worcester, MA Telegram called to my attention Peter Fisk's fever dreams. Lastly, The International Association for the Study of Dreams has been central to dialog in which I participated about COVID-19 dreams recently, and about dreams in general over the years. If you are not familiar with their publications, local and international conferences, and website, do explore www.asdreams.org which offers a wealth of resources for exploring the dreamworld.

About the Author

Deirdre Barrett, Ph.D. is a psychologist on the faculty of Harvard where she teaches courses on dreams to undergraduates, psychiatry residents & psychology interns, and lectures on hypnosis. She is Past President of both the International Association for the Study of Dreams and The Society for Psychological Hypnosis. She has written five books including *Pandemic Dreams The Committee of Sleep,* and *The Pregnant Man: Cases from a Hypnotherapist's Couch.* She is the editor of four additional books including *Trauma and Dreams*. She is Editor-in-Chief of the international journal, *DREAMING.* Dr. Barrett has published dozens of academic articles and chapters on dreams, hypnosis, sleep talking, and evolutionary psychology. Her current work focuses on dreams and creative problem solving and on lucid dreaming.
Dr. Barrett's commentary on dreams has been featured on Good Morning America, The Today Show, CNN, Fox, and The Discovery Channel. She has been interviewed for dream articles in *The Washington Post, The New York Times, Time, Life,* and *Newsweek.* Her own articles have appeared in *Psychology Today* and *Scientific American.* Dr. Barrett has lectured at Esalen, the Smithsonian, and at universities around the world.

Deirdre Barrett's website is www.deirdrebarrett.com

Her Instagram username is deirdre_barrett_dreams

Made in the USA
Las Vegas, NV
11 November 2021

34237381R00051